William Russell Smith

Was It a Pistol?

A Nut for Lawyers

William Russell Smith

Was It a Pistol?
A Nut for Lawyers

ISBN/EAN: 9783337404277

Printed in Europe, USA, Canada, Australia, Japan

Cover: Foto ©Suzi / pixelio.de

More available books at **www.hansebooks.com**

Æ PISTOL?

A NUT FOR LAWYERS.

TO THE

PRESIDENT OF THE BAR ASSOCIATION

OF THE UNITED STATES

THIS BOOK IS FRATERNALLY INSCRIBED.

What constitutes a judge ? Some stone,
Much gristle and a stiff back-bone.
Learning, and honesty combined
With soul and sentiment refined
Above all dross ; above all gold ;
Not to be bought, not to be sold ;
An ear for patience, and an eye
Quick to detect a sophistry ;
Serene of thought and apt of wit
T' expound the law just as it's writ ;
Without the power to see or know
Which is the friend, or which the foe ;
A solid bulwark lodged between
Innocence and the guillotine ;—
Give me that man to try my cause,
Just such a judge as DANIEL was.

CONTENTS.

WHAT IS WIT?

———

" Sometimes it lieth in pat allusion to a known story, or in season-
" able application of a trivial saying, or in forging an apposite tale.
" Sometimes it playeth in words and phrases, taking advantage from
" the ambiguity of their sense, or the affinity of their sound. Some-
" times it is wrapped in a dress of humorous expression : sometimes
" it lurketh under an odd similitude. Sometimes it is lodged in a sly
" question, in a smart answer, in a *quirkish reason*, in a shrewd imita-
" tion, in cunningly diverting, or cleverly retorting an objection.
" Sometimes it is couched in a bold scheme of speech, in a tart irony,
" in a lusty hyperbole, in a startling metaphor, in a plausible recon-
" ciling of contradictions, or in *acute nonsense.* Sometimes a scenical
" representation of persons or things, a *counterfeit speech*, a mimical
" look or gesture passeth for it : sometimes an affected simplicity,
" sometimes a presumptuous bluntness, giveth it being. Sometimes
" it riseth from a lucky hitting upon what is strange, sometimes
" from a crafty wresting obvious matter to the purpose. Often it
" consisteth in one knows not what, and springeth up one can
" hardly tell how. Its ways are unaccountable and inexplicable,
" being answerable to the numberless rovings of fancy and wind-
" ings of language.

" It is, in short, a manner of speaking out of the simple and plain
" way (such as reason teacheth and proveth things by), which, by a
" pretty, surprising uncouthness in conceit or expression, doth affect
" and amuse the fancy, stirring in it some wonder, and breeding
" some delight thereto."—ISAAC BARROW.

WAS IT A PISTOL?

THE TESTIMONY AND DEFENCE.

John Anderson, a farmer boy,
(Like other lads he had his toy)
Was charged with toting, if he did,
A pistol in his pocket hid.

The judge was there, the jury sworn,
The prisoner looking all forlon;
The witness swore (a woman stout)
She saw the pistol sticking out—
"Out of his pocket, just this fur "—
Measuring her hand—"from here to here;
About three inches, I should say,—

And this was on the Sabbath day;
We had a singing up at Zion,
Where we uns then were all a-gwine."

"How could you see it if concealed?"
"Well, John, at Sugar-creek, he kneeled
To get a drink, and as his skirt
Flopped up, I saw it plain as dirt."

"And in this county, and this year?"
"You bet it was, for that I swear."

Now every eye was turned upon
The prisoner, John Anderson,
As there he sat with curious eye
Twinkling betwixt a laugh and cry.
John rose up awkwardly and slow,
And asked to say a word or so.
"Yes, make your statement, little man,
And clean your skirts up if you can."

"I carried it," the prisoner said,
"To please the gals; I allers led
The music with my little Joe,—
My little forty pi-a-no.
I've got it ready just to show,
The very same the witness saw "—
And John prepared his gun to draw.
"An't please the Court, I'd like to show it;
Perhaps the witness still may know it."
And then he drew the pistol cu⁺,
And showed three inches of the spout;
Then asked the witness by her name
Whether or not it was the same.
"The very same!" exclaimed the dame,
"I'll swear it till the rats go tame !"

Then gravely towards the Court the boy
Turned to make profert of his toy.
"Suppose this pistol doesn't shoot,
And makes no noise above a toot ?"

"No matter," said the judge, "my son,
Our Court of Error holds it 'gun.'"
"Suppose it be a wooden gun,
And only carried round for fun ?"
"No matter," said the judge, "my son,
Our Court of Error holds it 'gun.'"
"Without a pan or frizzen in't,
And nary cock to hold a flint ?"
"No matter," said the judge, "my son,
Our Court of Error holds it 'gun.'"
"And s'posen there's no trigger here,
And that she only goes by air ?"
"No matter," said the judge, "my son,
Our Court of Error holds it 'gun.'"
"Supposin' that it ain't no pistol,
And nothin' but a 'Hickory Whistle' ?"
"No matter," said the judge, "my son,
Our Court of Error holds it 'gun.'"

"I'll show you how I make her bark ;

Just listen and you'll hear her, hark !''
Then to his mouth the furious boy
Applied the deadly looking toy,
As if all resolutely bent
To use the bloody instrument,
There in the court, to end the strife,
And desperately close his life.

The sheriff stood with goggle eyes,
The petrefaction of surprise.
That female witness cried: '' O John !
Don't shoot yourself, John Anderson !''
'' I'll show you how I let her go ''—
And then he made a toot or so;
Gently at first, and soft and low
As Eve's first sigh at her first woe;
Then whistled long and whistled loud,
As whirlwinds ripping through a cloud !

Up to their feet the jury sprang !
With shout and laugh the Court House rang.

>

The judge fell back, as in a trench,
And put his boots up on the bench,
And there amidst th' unbroken glee
Held high judicial jubilee.
The boy as if by demons led,
Or some dark inspiration fed,
Refused to stop th' infernal strain,
But blast on blast, in wild refrain,
Blew " Dixie," "Yankee Doodle " and
" Hail, Hail Columbia, Happy Land ! "
Then with a hand on either hip,
He broke out with "Old Zion's Ship."
And blew, as Gabriel blows for corses,
Or ——————— neighing for "WHITE HORSES! "

THE JUDGE'S CHARGE TO THE

JURY.

THE JUDGE'S CHARGE TO THE JURY.

The judge at last himself composes;
Drives from his face the clustered roses;
Sits upright in his easy chair,
Assuming a judicial air;
Fastens his eyes upon the jury,
Some lamb, some lion and some fury!
'Twas clear to every eye the judge
Considered the defence a *fudge;*
Having no mind to see the state
Bamboozled at so cheap a rate,
He tried to show the men before him
The prisoner's guilt, and how to score him.

"You know this is a crying evil;
It does more to stir up the Devil
Than all the ills in all the nations,
Except '*disturbing* Congregations;'
Now, these two things are quite enough to
Break kingdoms up, and do it rough too.

"Doubtless it is a great relief
To be unloaded of a grief,
As donkies, lightened of their sacks
And turned upon luxurious racks
Devouring fast, forget the goad
And all the up-hills on the road.
And so the pleasure too is great
To lift away another's weight;
As priests enjoy a mild content
When they absolve the penitent:
Sweet is the feeling to be kind,
To banish sternness from the mind;
As smiles delight in chasing down

The sullen, unrelenting frown;
Forgiveness is the road to bliss,
If all the other paths we miss;
But juries, when the law is broke,
Must rise superior to a joke;
Nor be decoyed by song or wit
Into a verdict of acquit."

OF JURIES GENERALLY.

"Juries were made for mighty things;
They first divided power with kings;
Held back the tyrant arm intent
To come down on the innocent;
Stood 'twixt the headsman and the block,
And planted freedom on a rock:
Proclaiming there th' immortal plan:
'MEN SHALL ADJUST THE RIGHTS OF MAN."
Juries can populate 'Sing-Sing,'
By taking boodlers on the wing;
Detect the counterfeiter's pen,

And 'rout the usurer in his den;
Take charge of commere on the seas;
Frown down the quibbler and his pleas;
Can force the judge to square his shoes,
And look out for his P's and Q's;
These artful suicides can die
And live again upon the sly,
Refuse to hang, by being hung,
And burn in turn the slanderer's tongue.''

OF THE DUTIES OF JURIES.

"A jury may discriminate,
But not too much against the state;
In leaning, if you lean at all,
Lean to the state, and prop its wall:
A state that loses once its level
Is on the high road to the Devil;
And wheresoever goes the state,
The people follow, sure as fate.
The state can expiate no sins;

Intangible, she feels no pins ;
However hard you kick or cuff her,
The people 'tis that have to suffer :
So, equally she's fire-proof,
And does not fear the Devil's hoof ;
And if the state should go to Hell,
(The same being indestructible)
The devil there, as you may learn,
Will seize on *something* that *will* burn :
And so 'tis clear to every eye,
The people 'tis that have to fry.
Stick to the state, enforce the laws,
If you'd escape the Devil's claws.

"Compassion !   That is very nice
And still commands its market price ;
For pity deluges the eye,
Makes blind and tends to mystify ;
Judgment perverted by a tear,
Is hood-winked justice, that is clear ;

So, MERCY, always rated high,
Whether you wish to sell or buy,
And *vice versa*, rated cheap,
(The drachmas coined the while you weep)
And, strange to say, the higher the price is,
The less she calculates the vices !
Mercy does more in her sweet way
To cheat the jailer of his fee
Than any known commodity ;
She makes more felons in a day
Than fleets e'er brought from Germany ;
Not Italy, with her stilettos,
Nor brigand Spain could so beset us :
When Pity and Compassion join,
And Mercy closes up the line,
To form a corner 'gainst the state,
(As ruffians do to run up wheat)
The Constitution sinks beneath
The ponderous weight and loses breath.''

The judge sat back an inch or so,
To let his cogitations grow;
As struggling with a ponderous train
Of great thoughts clambering up his brain;
Then, leaning forward with a bright eye,
Uttered thoughts luminous and mighty:

" What staple fills our daily sheets ?
Elopements, suicides, and cheats;
Murders, assaults and batteries—rape,
And crimes of every name and shape
Astound the sense and meet the eye;
Over the land these wind-sheets fly,
Cyclonical in shape and fury,
And killing more than they can bury !

" You hear of STRIKES thoughout the land,
With titled chieftains in command !
These MASTERS of the situation
Are simply curses to the nation !

Who's Thunderly, and whence his power?
What legal act makes him a tower?
What autocrat has signe1 his papers,
Enabling him to cut high capers;
Put prices up and down, and barter
Labor and beef without a charter?

" Coal miners, railroad engineers,
With mischief-making foreigners,
Plotting together, hedge the laws;
Anarchy claps her wings and caws,
And Robbery gripes with crimson claws!
These are big evils, but no bigger
Than may come from a PISTOL's trigger.
These must be stopped, but who's to stop 'em
If juries shirk the jobs, and drop 'em?

OF GUNS GENERALLY.

" It makes no difference at all
About the gun's material;

Whether of paper, lead or iron,
If human life it doth environ;
The law embraces, and it ought to,
Whatever implement may slaughter.
A whistle still may be a gun,
At least by implication;
For even an over-blast of breath
Is capable of causing death;
And life's the same if piped away,
As if 'twere taken in a fray :
A horn, some thousands years ago,
Blew down the walls of Jericho ;
And don't it often come to pass
That men are whistled off by gas ?
And that, too, when their dreams, perhaps,
Seem sweetest in elysian naps ?

" When paper wheels drive railroad cars,
May paper guns not rule the wars ?
And is it not our daily boast
2P

That paper ramparts guard our coast ?
' The day has come,' cries every sage,
' The ever blessed pasteboard age :—
' All paper—rails, wheels, cars and all !
' Bastion and moat and arsenal.'

" To-day we have a hickory flute ;
Is that to strike a jury mute ?
Next court we'll learn another lesson,
And see a paper 'Smith & Wesson.'

" A gun, whatever it is made of,
Is still a thing to be afraid of ;
In fact. the less it seems a gun,
The mightier mischief may be done,
Just as when ambuscaded armies
Turn up where no expected harm is ;
Or as, when Sin's less like the Devil,
The less you guard against the evil !

" Some think a gun, if broke in two,

Is not a gun in legal view,
Because, its parts being thus asunder,
It is incapable of thunder :
Our Court denies that this is true,
And holds to the sublimer view,
That, even though broken into flinders
And burnt, there's danger in the cinders !
As lightning has been known to come
Out of a voiceless vacuum !

" Suppose a pistol carried round,
Its parts in different pockets found ;
The barrel in the boot, the hammer
Hid in the vest, clean gone the rammer ;
The handle in the breeches' pocket,
Disjointed so you couldn't cock it ;
The tube chuck full of rust, the trigger
Minus its rivets ;—still, with rigor
And consummate judicial vigor,
The Court will pick up bit by bit,

To show you how the parcels fit !
And there you'll have before your faces,
The very gun the Code embraces !

" A gun may have a rusty lock,
And stubbornly refuse to cock ;
But many a lad is killed in fun,
By tampering with a rusty gun !
What mellows wine will mellow powder ;
The rust but makes the gun go louder ;—
And still, the older that the load is,
It mangles worse the stricken bodies.

A watch with broken spring (altho'
You shake it and it will not go)
Is still a watch, at least, for show ;
A coffee-pot may leak, and not
Be any less a coffee-pot,
Because it lets the liquid out
Some other way than through the spout !

You've heard about the jointed snake?
How into parcels it will break
If you but touch it, and again
Relink itself and whole remain !
And so, a snake, altho' it break
In parcels, it is still a snake !

CONCERNING THE PRISONER'S STATEMENT.

" The law allows, in lenient grace,
The prisoner to state his case ;
But statements thus by prisoners made
As proof is of uncertain grade ;
You may believe it, and you may
Cast it entirely away ;
' Tis nothing but his word o' mouth,
Without the sanction of an oath ;
And tho' the prisoner lies, he's free
From any taint of perjury ;—
For such equivocal obliqueness
Is charged up to the flesh's weakness.

THE STATUTE.

" This statute is a curious nut,
Viewed in whatever light ' tis put ;
It was much easier to make it,
Than ' tis for jurymen to crack it ;
For in its high judicial sense
It is and is not evidence !
It wears two faces the same day,
And yet, it don't look either way;
It gives the prisoner lots of chances
To raise emotional romances;
But then, if you detect a sham,
It isn't worth a—Jersey clam.
And here's the place t' adjust your eyes
And guard yourselves against surprise;
As jugglers have been known to kill
Alone by necromantic skill,
And people have been slain by glee
And laughed into eternity.

"Observe, the witness has admitted
(But witnesses may be outwitted)
The thing he claims to be a whistle,
The same thing that *she* thought a pistol:—
Now, this may take the question out
Of certainty, and breed a *doubt;*
But that depends upon the gumption
The jury brings to weigh presumption.
A man may whistle very well,
And still be on the road to Hell,
As ORPHEUS in the olden time
Fiddled his way to Pluto's clime.

THE REASONABLE DOUBT ELABORATED.

"Things may be proved by roundabouts,
Beyond all reasonable doubts;
But then, that reasonable doubt is
Perplexing as a fox's route is.
You must not fly around on wings,
Searching imaginary things;

Inquiring if the moon have peoples,
Or if the churches there have steeples.
And if this doubt be hard to find,
It should not sway the juror's mind;
For, if you have to cast about
To find it, 'tis a trumped-up doubt,
Not such as lets the prisoner out.

" A doubt is sometimes large, or small,
It is, and it is not at all;
You think you see, but do not see,
So dusky grows the mystery.

" When you go to the steeple-chase,
You *doubt* which horse will win the race;
You put your money on the best
And finest looking, for the test;
When you select your favorite horse,
You think you're leaving off a worse;
But then the one in sorriest plight

Beats all the others out of sight;
Up goes your money like a kite,
And you're the victim of a bite!
Now, these are fancy's doubts, not legal,
No more than Thespian crowns are regal ;
They have no substance on their faces,
And make no *prima facie* cases ;
The doubt must be a real doubt ;
In fact, it must be sticking out ;
A thing that reason can espy,—
Not a mere whimsicality ;
Must grow out of the self same facts
That constitute the prisoner's acts
And circumstances thereunto
Belonging, really and true,
As much a parcel of the case
As nose and eyes are of a face !

"Some say ' this world will ne'er look bright
Unless you set your glasses right,'

But there be things you cannot see
However clear your glasses be;   :
The little nothings that so flit
Behind a cunning woman's wit;   ✦
In these, 'twas never meant the eye
Of mortal man should curious pry;
For these be doubts the more you gaze on,
The more the mystery takes the haze on;
And so you'll find, the more you seek
To read the book, the more 'tis Greek.

"The angler's art exemplifies
Some dim and occult mysteries;
Let me explain without a quibble
The odds betwixt a bite and nibble:
The bite's a fact,—the nibble is
Much in the nature of a quiz,—
This nibble is a real *doubt*,
For if you jerk you catch no trout!

And so the habits of a flea
Make *it* a thing of mystery ;
For when you put your finger on
Th' accomplished acrobat, he's gone !
Just so, the sunshine on the floor
Goes out if you but shut the door ;
The shadows on the wall take flight
Whenever you snuff out the light ;
And rainbows, though they charm the eye so,
Won't let you bag 'em if you try to.

"And when an acrobat, who swings
And floats without the aid of wings,
High up in air, (you know the higher
He walks the less you see the wire)
Loses his equipoise, and nearly
Tumbles (a trick to fool you merely)
Till he recovers from the feint,
The fans stand still, and women pant;
But when in equipoise completely

He whirls about and walks back fleetly,
Asserts himself, with breast expanding,
You saw him falling, see him standing,—
You shout, in your enthusiasm,
'If birds have wings, that fellow has 'em.'
Now, here's the place to travel slow;
Let your imagination's glow
Subside; then ask the question, whether
The human arm e'er sprouted feather?
A feather's an essential thing
In the construction of a wing;
For without that material
There can't be any wing at all."

At this last simile, tho' pointed,
The judge's mill-rocks got disjointed;
And here his Honor,—while his eye
Took in the jury on the sly
To see if he had made things plain—
Charmed by the click of his own brain,

Exhibiting an earnest glow
Of satisfaction on his brow,—
Paused—but an expert in men's faces,
To catch perplexity's pale traces,
Could see at once the judge was stuck—
As losing his poetic pluck—
Stuck in the mazes of his fancies,
Stuck, in his own wild wire-dances,
Perhaps the first of his romances:
The Muse admonished him to skip
The enchanting theme, and let her rip;
But he resolved to hold his grip,
And Phœbus fired his upper lip !

Now John was skilled in many arts;
The people wondered at his parts;—
He could do anything, a'most,
At any time, at any post;—
Accomplished in ventriloquism;

However wise the crowd, he'd quiz 'em,
Thus oft inspiring wild commotion,
While none could see his lips in motion ;
So, while the judge was thinking how,
With straining brain and knotted brow,
And wondering where'n the devil he
Could find another simile,
A voice outspoken in the crowd,
Uttered this query, long and loud :
" I'd like to know, your Honor, whether
Some birds can't fly without a feather ?
Our bats *up here* have wings of leather."
 "Who's that ?" exclaimed the judge, up-
 starting ;
Rage in his stormy eyes out-darting ;
" Order !" exclaimed the sheriff, sneezing ;
When all the crowd 'gan muffled wheezing.
The jury, they sprang up in awe,
Gazed wildly round, but nothing saw ;
No answer came ; th' intensest ear,

With hands behind, stood out to hear ;
And wondering eyes ran round to see
If they could solve the mystery.—

No answer came.

When all were seated,
The ghost in muffled tones repeated :
" _Our_ bats _up here_ have wings of _leather!_ "

Now, while the judge, with lips apart,
Cast round him many a flaming dart,
The ghost continuing, seemed to say,
And in a most triumphant way :
"And don't some squir'ls skeat through the air
With nothing on their wings but _hair ?_"

The judge sank, limbering, in his chair,
And panted some, hornsnoggled there !
Undoubtedly his Honor felt
Disgruntled ;—thinking that he smelt

Brimstone, or something of the sort,
He ordered RECESS in the court ;
Told all the officers on post
To hunt up that infernal ghost,
And bring before him, man or devil,
The perpetrator of the evil.

THE RECESS.

3

THE RECESS.

The judge descended from the bench,
And stepped across the street to—quench.
The sheriff and his deputies,
Each having fight within his eyes,
Lifted their cudgels up and went
Around with desperate intent;—
The jury, some put on their hats
And looked around for *squir'ls and bats*,
Their heads already brimming o'er
With mystic doubts and legal lore;
The lawyers laid aside their briefs;
The prisoners half forgot their griefs;
Gay Merriment was monarch crowned,
And many a joke went reeling round.
And many a wink with glint and leer

Was cast towards the prisoner.
John was serene, but still looked shy,
Out of one corner of his eye;
Then, thinking he was free to go
And recreate as others do,
Pulled out his trusty little " Joe,"
And gave a gentle toot-a-too.
John then assumed the judge's chair,
Looked round with autocratic air,
Commanded in judicial tone
" Silence in Court," then tooted on.

O! 'twas a splendid sight to see
The antics of that revelry;
Alike ran wild the young and old;
That music made the timid bold;
The accents of that little " Joe "
Was grease for a rheumatic toe;
It lubricated hip and thigh,
And fired anew the dimmest eye;

There gray-beards, come to hear the law,

And whet anew some ancient *saw*,

Relax their muscles, and begin

To grin and dance, and dance and grin.

The people, masters of the hall,

Got up a general caterwaul;

While John, from lower notes to higher,

Called demons up to join the choir;

And showed the folks, as they applauded,

What Joe *could* do when he was crowded.

In mimicry he showed his skill,

Could mock a dog or hog at will;

Play waltzes, marches, dances, jigs,

And squeak like one or many pigs;

Out-" mew " the most accomplished cat;

Screech like an owl, hum like a bat;

Twitter like mocking-bird, and fill

The forest with poor "whip-poor-will,"

Then charge the jury like his Honor,

And fling his voice from any corner.

THE COURT REASSEMBLES.

THE COURT REASSEMBLES.

The judge came back; that he'd struck 'ile,
Was clear from his expanding smile;
He looked around, then beamed a boom
All over the capacious room;
Then told the sheriff to hand in
That ghost as he'd commanded been.

"I've looked around," the sheriff said,
Then, seemed to say: "the Devil's dead!"
As these last words appeared to float
Right from the sheriff's lips and throat,
The judge was startled;—while the sound
In traveling accents roared around;
"The Devil's dead; the Devil's dead."
"I'm not so sure," his Honor said.

·· He can't be found," the sheriff cries—
·· I'm here !   La ! how that sheriff lies ! "

Then thought forsook that sheriff's head,
And light from out his eye-balls fled !
Trembling he reeled, all limp and slack,
Without a back-bone in his back !
The people then began to wriggle,
And John could scarce suppress a giggle;
While gravity itself half frowned,
And open laughter roared around.

But now, the judge turns round and squares
Himself, and on th' assembly glares.
He seemed inclined to scold, and yet,
As halting 'twixt a freeze and sweat,
Half smiled, and casting off his fury,
Fixed the attention of the jury.

The judge seemed puzzled to begin;—
He had forgot to stick a pin

In his discourse where he left off,—
And so he hem'd and tried to cough:
But suddenly you might descry
A twinkle in his thoughtful eye;—
He'd caught the thread just where it broke,
And thus ingenuously spoke:
" I think that I was running out
My arguments about the *doubt;*
But since that time I've learned to know
That doubts come quick and go out slow.
Whether the Devil's here or not,
Invisible, but on the spot,
There is no shadow of a doubt:
You, gentlemen, must turn him out."

Emphatically this was said;
Then every juror wagged his head;
Which spoke as plain as heads could speak:
"We'll do't, you bet, the darned old sneak !"

THE JUDGE CLOSES HIS CHARGE.

" Admit that it is common sense,
To carry arms in self-defence,
This law denounces not as harm
Just the mere *carrying* of an arm;
For that would break, as you may see,
Our Constitution's guarantee;
The manner 'tis, and not the gun,
That this good law comes down upon.
'Tis the concealing of it in
The pocket—*that's* the mortal sin !
A man may carry, 'tis his right,
A dozen guns exposed to sight;
But while you may defend your life,
You sha'n't go romping round for strife;
Your hand still sweating on your knife, —
With grim death lurking there, and hid
Under your coat to kill some kid.

" Now take the case, and teach the boys

The tariff that you lay on toys.
It is not always that you can
Come plump down on the guilty man;
(Cunning and genius get away
With law and lawyers every day).
A burglar may defy the law;
Who picks a lock may pick a flaw;
Besides, 'tis thought a glorious sport
To break the law, and cheat the Court;
There're different ways of "striking 'ile";
Some dig the mines, some steal a pile;
No matter how the pile's acquired:
Who steals the most is most admired.
And who the cuteliest slips away,
Becomes the hero of the day.
　"So when you've got him, it is wise
To hold him up to people's eyes;
(Not merely as a sacrifice)
A light unhid by cloud or curtain,
To show that punishment is certain."

The jury then went out to find
If they were of the judge's mind;
T' inquire if they could see the law
Exactly as his Honor saw.

The prisoner he went down below
And took along his little Joe ;
Then, squatting on a cellar door,
Began again his strains to pour ;
While girls and boys, and cat and cur,
And every straggling villager
Drew nigh to hear the notes entrancing,
And all the town went drunk and dancing.

NOTE.—The jury is hung ! This is quite a surprise, considering the very elaborate and lucid charge.

As a consequence of this, the Court as well as the town is in a tumult of suspense and on the tip-toe of curiosity. In the meantime, in order that the reader may have some relief, we proceed to show how the indignant culprit took his revenge on the over-harsh judge.

THE CHARIVARI.

THE CHARIVARI.

Now, John had gumption—he could feel
The judge's leaning and his zeal;
Could see his Honor's doubled fist,
And how he sought the law to twist,
To make the jury bring him in
As guilty of this mortal sin;
And, as the clearer this he saw,
He felt a rising in his craw,—
A sort of grinding in his gizzard
To circumvent this learned wizard,
And punish such judicial quirking :—
And so he set his wits to working;
And how he gave bis Honor 'moses,'
You'll see before our story closes.
4P

THE JUDGE'S MOSQUITO FIGHT.

The judge, though battling hard all night,
Was beat in that mosquito fight;
And there lay sweltering,—vanquished quite;
Indeed, he was in woeful plight!
Floundering from side to side he rolled;
He had not slept an hour, all told;—
And now the eastern gates unbar
Their portals to the morning star;
Wing'd warriors, as he tried to doze,
Flew round, and lit upon his nose;
To that high promontory brought
Their forces,—there their battles fought;
Squadrons of liliputian size
Held carnival around his eyes;
Maneuv'ring on his face they swarmed;
And there their phalanxes they formed:
And thence th' infuriate legions stormed;
Some in the open field appeared;

Some ambuscaded in his beard ;
Some sought a more expanded place ;
(His ample forehead yields the space)
There, hid behind his sheltering brows,
They fit their arrows to their bows ;
Sharpen their beaks and whet their stings,
And furious flap their buzzing wings !
What visions ! Fifes and drums at hand !
While Gabriel seems to lead the band !

HIS HONOR SLEEPS.

Softly ! the judge begins to feel
The whirl of some revolving wheel ;
His half-sick fancy still pursues
His dream in its dissolving views ;
He sees, or rather thinks he sees,
The trees bow down, the nodding trees,
As courting some refreshing breeze ;
He hears, at least he thinks he hears,

The far-off music of the spheres,
Soft as the dirge in Cymbeline,
When Collins strikes the chords divine.

Softly ; he sleeps ; the window pane
Seems tinkling with the pattering rain ;
And from his roof, that seems to roar,
He hears the gliding waters pour,
As lambs flit round the sportive plain
And gambol at the moist refrain.

Softly : the shades are growing dense ;
That flock of sheep climbs o'er the fence ;
The rails and gate go whirling round,
And fainting daisies kiss the ground,
As HERMES comes with opiate wand,
And SLEEP with poppies in his hand.
O restless sleep, whence visions creep !
O silent sleep ! what king can keep ?
O balmy sleep when angels tread

Around the consecrated bed,
Make curtains of their wings outspread,
And perfume o'er the slumberer shed !

THE CHARIVARI.

But hist ! what fearful flout was that ?
The judge exclaims : " Drive out that bat !
"O mercy !"—
           " Mew "—
                          Then came a plunge !
And then a squall, and then a lunge !
Fearful the tussle that ensued !
Puss seemed to fly, but fierce pursued !
TOM telescoped the judge's dream,
At two quick bounds and one wild scream !
Loud as the throttle's scalding notes
When locomotives clear their throats !

Upright in bed his Honor sits,

As one not sure if right his wits ;
Listening, he hears the attempted flight,
The wails of the receding fight !
While squall on squall, in wild refrain,
Torture his ears and rack his brain.
Silence ! a moment : ah, how sweet !
Over his head he drags the sheet—
That ruffled judge, and tries to sleep,
While goblins through the curtains peep !—
Closed are his eyes, but panoramas
Display inexplicable dramas ;
While portents, comical and tragic,
Swing round in all the hues of magic,

The caterwauling dies away ;
What is it that renews the fray ?
At first a squeal, and then a squeak ;
A pig—a pig, that little sneak,
Prowling to gain an entrance fails,
And finds his head between two rails,

Fastened, he chokes and squeals in turns ;
Then comes the mother sow, and churns
Her grinding jaws in furious growl ;
While forty porkers swell the howl !
Then suddenly, upon the hogs,
Appeared to spring a dozen dogs !
With yelp and bark of cur and hound
Unbroken by a change of sound.

'Twas queer, all this concentrate roar
Was just beneath the judge's floor !
As sure as living, he could feel !
The jar below was palpable !
But now they cease, dog, hog, and porker !
While something here betrays the JOKER !
The pig continues still to squeak,
With variations, so to speak.
The judge, he thought, "there is some *jig*
Mixed in the squeaking of that pig !"
Then listening closer, plainly heard

That " Hickory whistle."

                    " By my beard !"

Upsprang his Honor—pushed the blind
Aside, looked out, but failed to find
Pig, hog or dog of any kind.
No living creature round about !
" Beyond all reasonable doubt
That's John, th' infernal Necromancer !"
Then, face to face, he had his answer;
JOHN peeped around the adjacent corner:
" Mo'nin', good mo'nin' to your Honor."

NOTE.—The jury still being unwilling or unable to agree,
we are bound to hang up our Harp.

But the situation is very unpleasant, inasmuch as the en-
raged judge is now holding parley with the prisoner for an
alleged contempt of court in the matter of the SERENADE.
We shall see what we shall see.

WAS IT A CONTEMPT?

WAS IT A CONTEMPT?

Our JUDGE he was a jolly wight,
Especially when out at night,
Having his fun amongst the boys,
And scooping all the transient joys;—
Was fond of Bacchus and his cup ;
But sometimes got his dander up.

This morning he was in a fury ;
And so (still waiting for the jury)
He called the prisoner to the bar,
And opened on him savage war :
" You have been guilty of contempt
From which all judges are exempt :
It is a rude insult to Court,
To make its Judge a thing of sport."

Now John felt queer when thus arraigned,
But gravely rose up and explained:

THE PRISONER'S SPEECH.   (APOLOGETIC.)

"Be not in haste to be offended,
Nor take insult when not intended;
For many a thing is done in joke
Not meditated to provoke;
And he who would most happy live
Must not be over-sensitive.

"Some folks are ever on th' alert
To have their precious feelings hurt;
Suspicious, peering round for pins
To prick their over-tender skins;
And so, they're always feeling shocks
And dodging from erratic rocks,
As if th' infuriated Fates
Were flinging brick-bats at their pates.
And that's because the wit's awry,

And frenzied the dilated eye.
With cranky people such as these
The ' big-head ' is a sore disease ;
And when it gets good hold, be sure
That it is mighty hard to cure;
The head becomes a huge balloon,
And holds the world as its saloon;
And when it reaches such a size,
A brick can't miss it if it tries.

" And here I claim the benefit
Of all the doubts that round us flit.
There's hardly anything that's certain
When it is done behind the curtain.
This world, however slow it runs,
Is full of ' Billy Pattersons '
That feel the jolt of many a lick,
And never know who flung the brick.

" There is no evidence that I

It was who made the varmints cry,
Except your high judicial guessin',
For I've been slow, you know, confessin':—
I've got one bit of legal wit,
And that is : never to admit."

THE COURT.

" But you had cobwebs in your hair;
Pray, tell me how you got them there ?
How came that mud upon your knee,
That any man that looks may see,
Except by prowling on all-four
Right underneath my chamber door ?"

THE PRISONER.

" As to the cobwebs in my hair,
I might have got them anywhere;
For in this easy-going town
They are the only things *full grown.*

" Under the floor's the place, I've heard,
Where ghosts do flee when they get scared;—
Now say, how does your Honor know
But that some ghost made all the row ?
For everybody knows they're awful
To do things wicked and unlawful.

" As to tha mud upon my knees,
Just hear me, if your Honor please :
You know the Lord will often try us
To find out if we are truly pious;
Now, being bowed down with many sorrows
And worked into a spell of horrors,—
With these sore troubles on me laying,
The honest truth is,—I'd been praying!"

At this the JUDGE relaxed a peg;—
He thought the prisoner meant to beg;
The grim frown fading with a quiver
As the gall went out from his liver;—

While in the audience round about,
A merry, giggling laugh broke out.

　John's eye being wondrous quick to see
　　things,
Keen to detect the veriest wee-things,
He saw the Court's relaxing rigor,
And seized upon 't with earnest vigor;
He felt his legs, no longer limber,
Run strengthening into stiffer timber;
Bracing himself from heel to shoulder,
He struck out in a tone much bolder,
And plunged with resolute intent
Into the central argument:

　" What constitutes an arsenal?
One single gun, and is that all?
And pray what constitutes a fort?
A pile of dirt heaved high in port?
What makes a synod? One poor priest

To look wise waiting for the rest?
What makes a Congress?   Tell me that?
One filibustering Democrat?
Or one colossal man from Maine?
What makes a Cabinet?   Jim Blaine?

" Now let's inquire a bit, what sort
Of thing is this you call a Court?
The MAN, he's but a part of it,—
The central figure, let's admit;
But still, besides the flesh and blood,
There's something holier understood;
And so, as it appears to us,
The Court is multitudinous.

"Whatever needs two things in making
Is not complete if either's lacking;
Without a nose and eyes in place,
There cannot be a perfect face:
It makes no odds if mouth and chin

Be there, and even the teeth to grin:
The thing is not at all complete,
And only a base counterfeit!
Now, what's a bell without a tongue?
Though in the highest steeple swung,
With forty sextons at the rope,—
It makes no sound to wake us up.

" Besides, a Court must ever be
On vigilance, with eyes to see;
With open scan and keenest peep;—
No Court can be allowed to sleep!
Will you contend with your great head
That COURTS can ever go to bed?
That Courts can shift, on mere pretence,
Their dignified habiliments?
And strip themselves to shirt and drawers?
Forbid the thought, ye legal powers!

"There must be guns to make a fort,

And officers to make a Court;
And chairs to sit on, and a place
For jurymen that try the case.
A court-house when the judge is gone
Is like a fort without a gun,
Or like a shell that's lost its snail,
Or like an eel without its tail;
Or like, (to whittle matters down,)
A circus that has lost its clown:
The better parts of each being gone
There is no life in either one.
So, without desk, and clerk and hall,
And sheriff there to scold and call,
There can't be any Court at all !

  " The MAN-part of the Court's exempt
In this high meaning of contempt ;
It is the hallowing around
That makes him walk on holy ground;
The high judicial function 'tis

That shields him from the arrow's whiz;
He's only sacred—seems to me—
In these habiliments of sanctity;
And when he lays these things aside,
The common lot he must abide;
And take his level, if he can,
With every other honest man.

"When he goes out to get his dinner,
He then becomes a common sinner;
When he goes down to get his supper
He takes the low grade—leaves the upper;
Or, when he goes to get a drink
And gives the tapster there a wink,
(Being quick to take an odorous hint)
And cocks his nose at scent of mint;
Comes down from his Empirium,
Leaves ether off and takes to rum;—
Whenever he sits down by me
To get his hog and hominy,

Was It a Contempt ?

At the same table, cheek by jowl;
Asks me to take a hot french roll,
And thanks me, plain as words can utter,
When I supply his plate with butter;
Politely asks to pass the sugar,
And mingles with me, 'hugger-mugger',—
He then asserts a worldly mind
And leaves his dignity behind.

" Now, I maintain, your Honor, then
There was no COURT there to contemn:
Observe: you weren't in any place
Commanding such judicial grace;
And not in any fix to be
Entitled to such sanctity;
For you had cut loose from the gown,
And laid the legal sceptre down;
You went round laughing at our jokes,
And rollicking with common folks;
Engaged at times in taking in

Mint-slings alternately with gin !
You didn't even *look* profound;
Your socks were lying loose around;
Your dress coat hanging on a chair;
Your night-shirt flopping in the air:
And the same nig' that polished mine,
Had taken *your* shoes out for a shine;
And I can prove, if called upon,
You didn't have your breeches on."

What happened then, there's hardly tellin',
Perhaps the roof and ceiling fell in:
The startled audience broke out yellin',
And even the sheriff, face to face
With judge and jury, fell from grace;
And seeing he couldn't quell the noise,
He cried out, " Go it—go it, boys;"
Then hung his hat upon his staff
And swung it round to excite the laugh !
The only thing that checked the squallers—

" I fine the sheriff fifty dollars,"
Exclaimed the judge, in roaring tone,
And brought his clenched fist clattering down!
This falling like a thunder bolt
Brought the wild people to a halt:
" And ten hours in the calaboose!"
And there they trotted off Ben Hughes!
Ben went along to punishment,
And swore he didn't care a cent.
" I'd throw my hat up out of reach,
To hear just such another speech;
I tell you, boys, that lad's a trump;
Our judge has run agin a stump."

And now, as every one must know,
Our JUDGE's face was in a glow;
In very truth it must be said
His Honor's face was more than red.
Indeed, he was quite ill at ease;
Took snuff—that failed to start a sneeze;

Then looked down on the prisoner,
And said, betwixt a frown and sneer:
"I've heard your speech, but cannot see
In it the least apology.
Intolerable insolence:
The speech is worse than the offence.
As vindicator of the law
I'm bound to make you come to taw,
And fine you fifty—"

                        "No, no, don't,—

Consider, judge:—I know you won't;
For mammy'll have to pay the fine,
And that'll take the last bright shine:
So we'd as well just shut up shop;
Our last was but a sorry crop;
With too much rain, and not enough,
(Now you may think this riddle tough)
We didn't gather stuff to do us,
Without a sheriff to pursue us.
We'll have no coffee for a year,

And no molasses, to make beer;
And Susan Jane will have to go
The winter without shawl or shoe.
Yes, everything we'll have to take
To market: everything we make!
The little gilt will have to go
Before she grows to be a sow;
The little porker must be kilt,
And ta'en to market, like the gilt;
Yea: even the eggs,—ah, who could ask it?—
Will go to fill the market basket:—
There ain't no profit sellin' eggs
Before they walk round on their legs;
For every egg of bird or chicken
Has feathers in it worth the pickin';
Some for a lady's fan, and some
To decorate the warrior's plume;
And some for softer, somnian uses,—
(For these, most men prefer the goose's;)
But you must wait until they sprout

Before you try to pluck 'em out.
Now, patience is a thing to brag on,
A wise man tarries for the wagon;
Nor loses time,—this roadside biding,
Gives many a tramp a rest in riding.

"I hope your Honor'll call a halt,
And give me nary nother jolt;
For I'm already upside down,
And couldn't find my way from town;
I hardly know right where I am,
For I feel shut up—like a clam.
You needn't feel the least surprise
If I go whistling through my eyes."

Now here the JUDGE pricked up his ears,
At the incipient creep of tears;
He brought his hand down on his desk
As if about to take a risk;
"Hold on! Hold on!" his Honor cries,

"I want no whistling through those eyes;
I've had enough of music, quite;—
In fact you've fairly won this fight!
You're just a very pink in blossom,
And here I take you to my bosom!
You've got the gift to clatter-claw,
And you're the chap to study law."

———

The JUDGE acknowledged the defeat,
The charge withdrawn, John took his seat.

———

The Court had nothing else to do,
Waiting the jury to pull through;
The sheriff in the calaboose,
Wild jollity again broke loose;
The prisoner, as in gratitude,
Offered the Court an interlude!
The judge relaxed his rigorous rule,
And generously "turned out school;"

Told Johnny to " leave out the pig,
And let us have a genuine jig."

Then John whipped out his little Joe,
And licked his lips, and let her go.

THE HUNG JURY.

THE HUNG JURY.

The jury, when they first went out,
Were much bewildered by the doubt;
In truth, the only fact they saw
Distinctly was the pistol law.
For that had been enacted by
The highest of authority;
And plain, for every eye to see,
To benefit society.

COONER'S SPEECH.

Sam Cooner, (on his face a scowl,)
Was looking wise as any owl,
Off in the corner where he sat,
Putting together this and that;
A-turning over in his head

The weighty things the judge had said
About the flea, and steeple-chases,
(For Sam was mighty fond of races,)
Sam thought the judge's speech well done
Until he struck the *paper gun*:
That was a staggerer, and so
Sam left the judge at Jericho;
At once embraced the prisoner's cause,
And squared himself t' expound the laws.
He couldn't bring his wits to see
A reason for the penalty !
When thus declaring his intent,
He broke out wild and eloquent:

"There's nary law in all the code,
However plain it is and broad,
But has a penalty to mate it ;—
Before you're bound to vindicate it
It must be broke,—or badly bent;
Or else, there is no punishment !
It's very good to make a law,

And very bad to break a law;
But, is it not an idiot's joke
To mend a thing before it's broke?"

Profound this ratiocination:
" Show me, " cried Sam, "the provocation!"
Now Sam looked round to get his answer.
No answer came, no, not a man, sir,
Will join in argument with Cooner:
He'd tackle Daniel Webster sooner !
Sam waited with his legs across,
But nobody assailed the boss.
He threw his left leg o'er the right,
But nobody would offer fight.

"You know the judge, he told us flat
That we must lean *towards* the state?
That ain't my doctrine, tho' it's his'n;—
I hold it just the rankest pyzen."

Sam changed his left leg back again,
6P

His high composure to maintain,
And manifest his earnest zeal
To vindicate the common weal.

JIM LINDSEY'S SPEECH.

Jim Lindsey looked up and declared :
" Them's just my sentiments, b'g-a-a-r-d;
I'll stick to Cooner 'gin the judge ;
They're mighty nigh, all of 'em, fudge.
They're allers sure to take a stand
Agin the poor men of the land;—
These fellers, when they git too high
Above the commonality,
Their eyes git mixed with lofty things,
And they go whirling round on wings;
They quit the ground and lose their mind,
And, giddy-headed, go it blind !
I vote to take 'em down some pegs."
Jim Lindsey spoke, and crossed *his* legs.

TOM SIMPSON'S SPEECH.

Tom Simpson said: " he'd say his say,
He didn't know much, any way;
But I'm for clearing ;—I'm agin
The law, and want to hedge 'er in.
If our old fathers carried guns
Without a fine, why can't their sons ?
The Constitution guards the right ;
You'll find it there in black and white,
As plain as printer's ink can make it;—
And even a squint-eye can't mistake it."

THE FOREMAN SPEAKS.

The foreman, as in duty bound,
Stood by the state, and spoke profound :
" But that's all over now, and we
Must stand up to the *new* decree
Made to protect society."

SIMPSON.

"I don't care for the new enact ;
The Legislatur,' it was packed
By lawyers, and such whipper-snappers,
On purpose, only to entrap us.
And what's SOCIETY,—ain't we
A part of that society ?
Now, agin any *such protect,*
I do most solemnly object."

THE FOREMAN.

"But we're not here to make the law,
Nor break it, nor to pick a flaw;
But to enforce it as it is,
Just as his Honor says it is.
We're bound to see, just as he sees
The law through his enlightened eyes."

COONER AGAIN :

"Admit the law, is that enough
To send an innocent prisoner off?
Are we assembled, just for fun,
To swear a hickory flute's a gun?
And don't we, if we so declare it
Not only say it is, but swear it?
I've blown a thousand of 'em, so
Has every single one of you.
Now look ye, men, boys will be boys,
And what are boys without their toys?"

TOM TATUM'S SPEECH.

Tom Tatum, he who taught the school
And measured everything by rule,
Stood up, and said in solemn tone :
"What constitutes a judge? Some stone,
Much gristle and a stiff back-bone.
Learning and honesty combined

With soul and sentiment refined,
Above all dross ; above all gold ;
Not to be bought, not to be sold ;
An ear for patience, and an eye
Quick to detect a sophistry ;
Serene of thought and apt of wit,
T' expound the law just as it's writ;
Without the power to see or know
Which is the friend, or which the foe ;
A solid bulwark lodged between
Innocence and the guillotine ;—
Give me that man to try my cause,
Just such a judge as DANIEL was."
Tom Tatum spoke, and took his seat ;
And Cooner clapped his hands, you bet.

BROTHER MILLS MAKES A PROPOSITION.

Now Brother Mills, a Methodist,—
He preached sometimes, sometimes played
  whist—

An unconvicted reprobate,
He always argued for the state,
Himself being guiltily inclined,
He thought 'twas so with all mankind—
Said: "Cooner, there is no denying
That you can beat in argifying ;
You're just the best I ever saw
When it comes down to jaw-for-jaw.
Whether the Lord supplied the gift,
Or Satan gave the Lord a lift
In making you so glib of lip,
I'll not inquire,—but let that slip;
And I'll not tackle you with words,
But I can *put you through at keerds;*"
And Mills pulled out a greasy deck,
And flapped 'em close to Cooner's cheek !
" I'll gamble my opinion
Against your stake if you'll stake John !
If I beat you, John guilty be;
If you beat me, then John goes free."

Cooner, impelled to show his grit,
Declared that he would take the bet
As far as his opinion went ;
But then, unless the rest consent,
You see, he couldn't undertake
To put the other men's at stake.

THE FOREMAN.

The foreman then he gave command,
"Let's vote, and see, men, how we stand;
And then each party may take side,
And let old 'Seven-Up' decide."
They balloted,—la : what a mix !
The jury still stood six to six !
Such was the fix, all night, all day ;
With no sign out of giving way.

OLE SLEDGE.

Then stood the parties side by side,

And all said : " Let the keerds decide,"
Excepting him that taught the school;
He said : " It went agin his rule,
He had a little conscience, he,
And would not give himself away."
And so he drew himself clean in,—
(You couldn't hardly see his chin)

Now, while the jury, hesitating,
Some half consenting, still debating,
Ben Hughes, — ah, never a better fellow,
Especially when a little mellow,—
Ben Hughes the sheriff came to see
If they were likely to agree.
The sheriff said to Cooner : " Sam,
(Keep your mouth closer than a clam)
I've brought along a little rye,
A good thing for a gummy eye ;
As you've been sitting up all night
I thought that you might like to try 't."

Then every eye, yea, twenty-four,
The four and twenty all got sore,
And couldn't see things worth a cent
Until they tried the liniment!
In this, not being over nice,
Some of the men applied it twice!
Till every one felt proud, and prouder,—
Such is the force of liquid powder.
Even the good school-master, he
Found *out* the *better* way to see ;
For when he bathed his *other* eye,
He peeped around like, on the sly !
Ah! you could see it in a twinkle !
The liniment wiped out a wrinkle !
Wrinkle by wrinkle disappeared ;—
The teacher's conscience, it was cleared;
So potent was the liniment
That smilingly *he* gave consent ;
And said (he'd been the only stickler)
" Play for it, boys, I'm not partickler."

Now Mills pulled down his cuffs, but Cooner
Rolled up his sleeves—true sign of honor.
You couldn't swear what Mills would be at,
But sly suspicion whispered che–at.
But Cooner, he stood solid there,
To win the game—upon the square.

Not keener glow men's eyes in battle,
Nor wilder stare the ox-eyed cattle
At scent of blood, in fear or fury,
Than those same eyes of that same jury,
Protruding for the bugle's call !
The school-master's out-glowed them all;
For he had staked more of his soul,
And dipped his conscience in the bowl.

Be 't known, there was no table there,
And not a solitary chair ;
The men sprang up from off the benches
And stood, like soldiers guarding trenches.

The champions straddled for the embrace,
With knee to knee, and face to face,
Quite near enough for mutual grip.—
" Now, cut for deal and let her rip."

Mills won the deal, the entering wedge
Of that hard knot, ycleped " Ole Sledge."
Mills shuffled long, and held 'em slack,
And innocently turned—a jack !

That jack of clubs appeared to be
The symbol of iniquity;
You saw it in the rascal's eye,
The very lust of knavery ;
He knew the touch of Mills' finger,
And when to bounce, and when to linger;
He stayed—just where Mills planted him,
And came—just when Mills wanted him.

Now Mills, he had the queen and king,

And trey to back the royal ring ;
While Cooner had the deuce and ace.
(But didn't show it in his face,)
And being inclined to try the bluff,
Says he : "I haven't got enough."

Successful bluffing's hard to work,
But long experience learns the quirk :
A solid nerve and stolid face
It takes to do the thing with grace ;
However brave you may appear
A keen eye will detect *some* fear ;
And when the less you seem to hope,
A keen nose scents the impending scoop.
Cooner repeated : " Mills, I beg,
And you must lift me up a peg.
Now give me one, or give me three,
It makes no difference to me."
The thing was very slyly done :
Said Mills : " I think I'll give you one."

When Cooner dropped his ace and deuce,
Mills thought the devil was let loose !
When Cooner showed high-low-gift-game,
The parson looked uncommon tame !
Cooner stood four to Mills' one !—
This seemed auspic-i-ous for John.

Cooner looked round with mild content,
And said : " Boys, pass the liniment.
I think the parson's eyes require
Another touch of that camphire."

Now, it was Cooner's turn to deal,
And he began the cards to feel;
In shuffling, he detected that
(And so he thought he smelt a rat)
One card—it had a ragged edge,
A thick and thin end—like a wedge,
And so, like Mills, he held 'em slack,
Manipulating of the pack,
Till he too *turned* the *self-same jack !*

At this, Bro. Mills looked just as if
He smelled some brimstone in that whiff !
While seeing the parson's eyes averted,
The jack himself seemed disconcerted;
Expressing in his countenance
Much sorrow at the queer mischance;
And so he smiled a smile that meant
That *he* was there by accident,
Entirely against his will,
Out-witted by Sam Cooner's skill !
Mills, he was wrathy with his saint,
But made no audible complaint;
And, being then incorrigible,
He voted jack to Pluto's stable.

'Twas Mills' beg ; he tried to show
That he was puzzled what to do.
He hesitated, as if reading
A knotty text before proceeding;
Looked glad and sorry, all the same;
And once seemed threatening to play 'm:

But then he paused—to scratch his leg,—
Concluding that he " *bleeved* he'd beg."
" Well, beg or not, it is your say,
I'm in no hurry anyway."
Then Mills looked on his hand again,—
" I beg," and Cooner said : "Amen,
I give, that makes you two, I'm five,—
Knock under, or be smoked alive."

Mills, having nothing to command
A single trick, laid down his hand.
Thus Cooner, 'mid a wild hub-bub,
Had won the first game of the rub !

The second game went on apace;
Mills played it with a brightening face :
His faithful jack again at post,
The luck was changed, and Cooner lost.

Now for the rubber,—that's the tug;—

Like bears impatient for a hug,
The lusty champions quick and hard
Gave emphasis to every card;
For you might hear their knuckles ring,—
The long bench answer'd echoing.

And now the game stands six to six,
With Mills' deal and Mills' mix;—
'Twas clear to every eye save Cooner's
That John was numbered 'mongst the goners !
When lo, that same jack takes his place,
And grins a grin in Cooner's face !

At this some disaffection sprung up;
Rebellion's banner, it was flung up;
The jury, they seem stultified,
And some of 'em look bugle-eyed !
But Cooner struck his swelling breast,
And thus the discontent suppressed:
7P

"We're bound in honor; it is right
To keep our plighted honor bright;
Now, boys, see here, the thing is done,
We must solidify as one;—
Like caucuses that nominate,
(Their business is to save the state,)
They fight and cuss and catterwaul,
Till one side, driven to the wall,
Cries quarter,—then they all combine,
And fall into the loyal line;
For still, the more they disagree
The closer friends they come to be;
And tho' they grow most clamorous,
And come to blows as they discuss,
They swear they are unanimous,
And come out shouting cheek by jowl;
Support the ticket heart and soul;
All holding up ONE 'simmon pole !
Now, let us march right into court
And give our verdict, as we ought."

And so the jury after awhile
Marched into court in single file,
And said as audibly as thunder:
" The prisoner's guilty." John went under.

Note.—The verdict was received with hisses by the audience. John said ut little. An old attorney who had been startled at the iniquity, suggested to the Court—"Amicus Curii,"
that the prisoner at this stage of the case ought, in justice, to
be advised that he was entitled to a lawyer, in order that he
might exercise, in technical form, his right to move the Court
to set aside the verdict and have a new trial, if there should be
any grounds,—and he ventured, with deference, to say that
there might be such grounds.

The Court, exuberant of good humor upon the finding,
readily consented to this, appointed legal counsel to take
charge of the prisoner's case, and graciously gave time for the
preparation of the motion, which was in due time filed, stating
numerous specific reasons for setting aside the verdict,
This motion, and the due consideration thereof, occupied the
whole of the next day, and will furnish abundant material
for another song.

THE JUDGE'S HOMILY.

TO THE PRISONER.

"Whene'er you meditate a sin,
And consummate by plunging in,
You'll learn at last, beyond a doubt,
It's easier getting in than out.
You travel gaily for a while
Until you find in *durance vile*
That you've struck fire instead of 'ile.
You look round for your patron saint,
Imploring him to hear your plaint:
But then you see, nor feel surprise,
That even he averts his eyes;
And leaves you sadly in the lurch,

Wailing betwixt the slums and church;
Without the ' benefit of clergy';
And there he'll hold you hard, and purge ye,
Till penitence commensurate
Appease the church as well's the state:
And so you'll find that you're not clean in,
Till the state dusts your fragrant linen;
(Or, if it's oznaburghs you've got on,
The state will fumigate your cotton.)"

www.ingramcontent.com/pod-product-compliance
Lightning Source LLC
Chambersburg PA
CBHW030540270326
41927CB00008B/1451